— GOD'S LOVE IS —
INCOMPARABLE

God Is Really Good

WISS JEAN-PHILIPPE

WESTBOW
PRESS®
A DIVISION OF THOMAS NELSON
& ZONDERVAN

Scriptures taken from the Holy Bible, New International Version®, NIV®. Copyright © 1973, 1978, 1984, 2011 by Biblica, Inc.™ Used by permission of Zondervan. All rights reserved worldwide. www.zondervan.com The "NIV" and "New International Version" are trademarks registered in the United States Patent and Trademark Office by Biblica, Inc.™

WestBow Press books may be ordered through booksellers or by contacting:

WestBow Press
A Division of Thomas Nelson & Zondervan
1663 Liberty Drive
Bloomington, IN 47403
www.westbowpress.com
1 (866) 928-1240

ISBN: 978-1-9736-2185-0 (sc)
ISBN: 978-1-9736-2194-2 (e)

Library of Congress Control Number: 2018902455

Print information available on the last page.

WestBow Press rev. date: 04/18/2018

Who is God?

Is there a difference between all that God has created?

Does God himself admit the difference in his creation?

Who is Satan?

How did God act?

Can you now make your choice and see the difference?

Your only solution is: "Come now!"

Let's do a little analysis on the points that we are coming to develop:

Where is the suffering coming from?

The consequences that may arrive to the ones that do not listen to the Eternal God's voice.

Analyze two more examples for better to make clear the big difference between the Flesh and the Spirit.

Would you rather follow Satan and disobey God?

How are we going to fight?

It doesn't exist, or it shall never exist another God as you my God!

We must love God

All the Glory is to God.

In comparison with man and lion.

What are you doing with the intelligence that God had gave to you?

How can we go away of the sin?

What's that God is waiting of us?

GOD'S PEACE HAS BEEN WITH YOU!

This is all a great pleasure for me to invite all my readers. **Believers/Christians** in **"God"** or the **Non-Believers/Non-Christians** in **"God"** to spend a little time with me. I do of manner to you own that you're going to have a good time that is pretty well enough with me at the field of the Holy scripture called **"The Bible"**. In doing this little turn in the field of the Holy scripture, **"The Bible"**, indeed we are going here to discover together:

> **Who is God?**

> **Is there a difference between all that God created?**

> **Does God himself admit the difference in his creation?**

Elsewhere, we are going to examine together how and why these subjects are set. Afterwards, we'll go to examine how **"God's Love is Incomparable,"** and plays a primordial part in our lives.

Let's go there together!

You are all cordially welcome in the field of the Holy God **"The Bible."** It is also important that, we first begin to pay attention to the very moment, we hold forward slowly at the heart at the field Holy of God "**The Bible**." Second, we can also have a better understanding of the contest that we are going to approach, on the following subjects:

Who is God?

Is there a difference between God's creation?

Does God himself admit the difference in his creation?

First off, we are going there to have great conspicuous without rumors and without the uprising hearsay. That means, each one of these conspicuous points are going to exactly justify across Biblical references. Moreover, each one of these conspicuous points are also going to justify from our daily experiences, just to provide proof for more full lights to ourselves. Rightly said that have been the first guests, and at everybody, especially above all those who have yet to hear the truth about who "**God**" is.

In fact, the outlining of my thoughts stipples all day on only the supreme name "**God**" for better conscientious analysis of this interesting subject, "**Who is God**". Indeed, as I invite you, thus I beg of you to also invite your family members and all your friends to read and analyze these little details together, which will be interesting enough, that will help reveal all the reasons to answer the question: **Who is God?**

The Holy Bible, the guide and the source of all God's knowledge, is going to help us to correctly answer the question that is stated above.

Everywhere else, that question would seem a little difficult to answer in the same way as for certain men/women of letters or scientists despite that they do often call them **"The**

Learned". If we can point out some among those who are right by universal acknowledgment such as:

Nicolas Copernic (Founder of the Cosmology Heliocentric)
//1473-1543

Johannes Kepler (Founder of the Astronomy Physical)
//1571-1630

Galilee (Founder of the Physical Experimental)
//1565-1642

William Harvey (Founder of the Medicine Modern)
//1578-1657

Robert Boyle (Founder of the Chemistry Modern)
//1627-1691

John Ray (Founder of the Biology Modern)
//1627-1705

Isaac Newton (Founder of the Classical Physical)
//1642-1727

Louis Pasteur (Founder of the Microbiology)
//1822-1895

William Thomson Kelvin (Founder of the Thermodynamics)
//1824-1907

Albert Einstein (Founder of the Physical
Theoretical Modern)
//1879-1955

The scientists that we are talking about are cited above in this article:

The most renowned Scientist of all time, believed in God!

Ref.: m. Alter info.net:

Indeed, they used all the resources known to try to find the origin of **God**, to know who or what He is. That has been to no purpose, because while all their resistance, they're not able to have their eyes opened while peering through their strong telescopes, hence they were not able to see, to understand, or to answer the question: **Who is God?**

"**The Bible**" yields plenty for those who are believers in **Jesus-Christ**, the answer is very clear and simple: "**God is Love**". (Ref. 1Jhon 4:7- 21). Before the mountains were born or you brought forth the whole world, from everlasting to everlasting you are God. Ref. **(Ps.90.2)**. *New International Version.*

Moreover, **God** is the one principal creator of the entire world. He has all the knowledge. He can build and destroy everything in one second when he would want. He is, the only God who has all the power to accomplish anything. His eyes can see everything. The **Bible** states: "The eyes of the Lord are everywhere, keeping watch on the wicked and the good. 4) The soothing tongue is a tree of life, but a perverse tongue crushes the spirit. 5) A fool spurns a parent's discipline, but whoever needs correction shows prudence. 6) The house of the righteous contains great treasure, but the income of the wicked brings ruin. 7) The lips of the wise spread knowledge, but the hearts of fools are not upright. 8) The LORD detests the sacrifice of the wicked, but the prayer of the upright pleases him. 9) The LORD detests the way of the wicked, but he loves those who pursue righteousness. 10) Stern discipline awaits anyone who leaves the path; the one who hates correction will die. 11) Death and Destruction lie open before the LORD-how much more do human hearts ". Ref. **(Proverbs 15:3,11)**.

All that means, that **God** is the only one who is masterful in life. He is the Alpha and Omega. **Revelation 1:8** "I am the Alpha and the Omega," says the Lord God, "who is, and who was, and who is to come, the Almighty". Moreover, "Things in heaven and on earth, visible and invisible, whether thrones, powers, rulers, or authorities; all things have been created through him and for him." Ref. **1 Colossians 1:16**

As stated in the **Holy Bible** of **Jehovah**: "For every house is built by someone, but **God** is the builder of everything." Ref. **Hebrews 3:4**.

In fact, **God** is the only person with great power, and reigns eternally. Indeed, the answer that becomes visible but reaches a higher level also hinders most people from clearly comprehending. That means, it needs to be very clear and simple, so that everybody can understand: **Who God is**?

Let us go into the fountain-head divine, the origin of the truth, which should allow us to always find the answer, the "**Bible**," where **God** himself has given the correct answer to **Moses**.

Firstly, listen what **God** said to **Moses** "I am the **God** of your father, the **God** of **Abraham**, the **God** of **Jacob**." At this, **Moses** hid his face, because he was afraid to look at **God**. Ref. **Exodus 3:6**.

Secondly, **God** said to **Moses**: "So now, go. I am sending you to Pharaoh to bring my people the Israelites out of Egypt." Ref. **Exodus 3:10**.

Thirdly, **God** said to **Moses**, "**I AM WHO I AM**. This is what you are to say to the Israelites: '**I AM** has sent me to you.'" Ref. **Exodus 3:14**.

Fourthly, **God** also said to **Moses**, "Say to the Israelites, 'The **LORD**, the **God** of your fathers-the **God** of **Abraham**, the **God** of **Isaac** and the **God** of **Jacob**--has sent me to you'. This is my name you shall call me from generation to generation." Ref. **Exodus 3:15**.

All the things that God created are perfectly **good**. And all those things that **God** has created are outstanding and are unique. Sometimes we ponder about, why **God** created evil among good?

My dear friends who come from here and everywhere, especially you who now read with me. Listen please, the **Bible** has already put all the answers to make our faith firm in **God**'s word. In the same way, the purpose of the **Bible** is to open our eyes, and our knowledge to the truth, that means, the **Bible** wants to <u>put all kinds of disquiet</u> that can torment our soul far from us. Please listen to how the **Bible** answers the question: Why did **God** create evil among good? "The **LORD** works out everything to its proper end-even the wicked for a day of disaster." Ref. **Proverbs 16:4**.

All those who believe in **God**, are those who are so smart. They are so smart because they can see and they can understand the different between the good and the bad. It's true that every Christian can tell you that **God** has all power in his hands. Everything he has did on the earth as on the heavens are wonderful. These are the reasons for which we must believe in **God** and only in him. Several reasons can be approved again why we must believe in **God** and only him.

Let us take these two examples:

a) Before and After all creation, there wasn't/ isn't a person who existed that could dare explain how **God** has done to realize this splendid world.

b) Today and until to the end of the time, we see that no person could dare to say or to testify how that **God** has created this wonderful Universe. Everyone (Christians or Pagan, in the same way for Satan) continue to enjoy all the works of **God**.

No one can explain the works of **God**, nor explain how they have been created. This continues to challenge everyone, and more specially for all the learned. In fact, I can't explain the works of **God**, because I don't have enough knowledge for that. Neither can I explain why everyone doesn't believe only in **God**. Everyone should believe in him, because **God** has proven to everyone that there is no one like him. There is no success for all those who don't believe in **God**...

> Me, I only believe in **God**.
> I only believe in **God**,
> because he has created me.
> I only believe in **God**,
> because he has created everything.
> I only believe in **God**,
> because he takes good of care of me every day.
> I only believe in **God**,
> because he takes good of care of me every night.
> I **only** believe in **God**,
> because he is my true **God**.
> I only believe **God**,
> because he is never a liar.
> **God** loves me.
> Tell me about you...
> Do you believe in **God**?
> If you don't believe in **God**
> Then, may you tell me...
> Oh, may you tell me,
> In who, or in what do you believe?
> It is unfortunate for all those who
> don't believe in **God**.
> Me, I believe....
> Yeah!!!
> I'm proud to tell you...
> That I only believe in **God**.

☞ DOES A DIFFERENCE EXIST BETWEEN GOD'S CREATION?

To the purpose, we can answer that the **Love of God** characterized by **God's** generosity or to valorize by **God's** extent that has been the **Supreme God**, of him, created all with great diversity.

Yes or no, is there a diversity in the existence of **God**'s work? That is the reason to which that the diversity of this difference is well notable in everything. And, this is what allows our heart to decide what he/she likes, prefers, or desires and with all the right choices. But, without any right to be rejected the right of what our heart doesn't like, because everything is good and perfectly good. The **Bible** states: "For everything **God** created is good, and nothing is to be rejected if it is received with thanksgiving." **Reference: Louis Second Bible. Ref. 1 Timothy 4:4**.

☞ ADMITTED GOD BY HIMSELF TO HAVE A DIFFERENCE IN HIS CREATION?

Everywhere else, it must be emphasized that **God** himself likes the variety, and **God** proved it, and He has accomplished it on every single creation. We believe that everyone has his likes and dislikes, so it must be the same for **God**. If we can consider these three examples following:

> **God** created the man which is different to the woman.

> **God** created all the beasts, each one of them are totally different.

> **God** created the plants, each one of them are totally different.

However, **God** gave to man the ability, that means, man can reflect, man can think, and analyzed before acting. On the other hand, **God** doesn't give to the beast that faculty of the reason. This aspect is also important to be said that the man is well off to enjoy his superiority in proportion to the beast as also all created things that are in the universe. If **God** has given the right to man to dominate over all created things is because **God** had already set the difference between the man and the beast. Therefore, we see that it's only the man who dominates without any limit on everything that is on the earth. Listen what **God** says: "Let us make mankind in our image, in our likeness, so that they may rule over the fish in the sea and the birds in the sky, over the livestock and all the wild animals, and over all the creatures that move along the ground." Ref. **Genesis 1:26**.

This question of difference becomes known as a tittle-tattle or a terrible disease that gnaws at the majority men's hearts in the world. Especially, every man who can't understand why **God** set up the difference in his creation, it is always the ones who question of the difference in a context that is contrary at **God**'s will. In fact, this terrible disease of interpretation about of the difference develops slowly but propagates at the innermost souls of everyone who makes the bad interpretation. Moreover, this terrible disease becomes infectious, influencing people from generation to generation.

In result, there is a breach of ethics among a category of people such that the people who like to think that they are superior to others. It becomes visible to see in our society how that either one or the other humiliate one another by false form of reasons such that: different skin color, money, physical body, beauty, sickness, knowledge, etc...

This breach of one's ethics is so considerable that it even destroys the good relationships that existed between human beings. By contrast, there aren't any Biblical references from whom show itself to us that **God** has given the right to a man to be superior than another man whatever skin color, money, physical body, beauty, sickness, knowledge, etc.

At first, **God** never accepted the terrible manner from which that man used to interpret the difference that he set up in his creation in the nature of things.

That's well understandable that all the misconstructions come from Satan. A question that we can ask: Who is Satan?

❧ WHO IS SATAN?

The Bible defines Satan clearly for us as an angelic being who fell from his position in heaven due to sin, and is now completely opposed to **God**, and he's doing everything in his power to fight against **God's** purposes. At the same time, Satan is becoming a dangerous influence on the children of **God**.

Moreover, Satan was also created by God as an Angel, indeed; he lived in the heaven as the Cherubim and God called him "Lucifer". Unfortunately, Satan sinned and was punished by God.

Moreover, Satan was also created by **God** as an Angel. After that Satan sinned and was punished by **God**, indeed; he lived in the heaven as the Cherubim and **God** called him "Lucifer".

"How you are fallen from heaven, O shining star, son of the morning! You have been thrown down to the earth, you who destroyed the nations of the world." Ref. **Isaiah 14:12.**

God gave everything to Lucifer but, Lucifer is a vicious angel that means he's not honest, therefore he came to be a lot more anxious to **God**. We can see that despite **God** giving everything to Lucifer, but Lucifer did not feel glad to see the other angels who adore **God**. So, Lucifer just wanted to have his own power or his own throne. In addition, Lucifer wanted to be same with the **Lord** who is the only creator.

Let's read this biblical passage together: "You said in your heart, I will ascend to the heavens; I will raise my throne above the stars of **God**; I will sit on the mount of assembly, on the utmost heights of Mount Zaphon. I will ascend above the tops of the clouds; I will make myself like the Most Higher. 15- But you are brought down to the realm of the dead, to the dead, to the depths of the pit." Ref. **Isaiah 14:13-15**

Here, we finish to discover who is Satan.

Satan is:
Ambitious
Hypocrite and Perfidious
Selfishness
Enemy of God
Death
Virus
Angel Rebel
Destructive
Liar
Spirit Malicious
Criminal
Deceiver
Copious
Crazy
Dishonest
Footpad
Persecutor
Darkness
Wicked
Foolish
Poor
Jealous

Tempter
Pollution
Poison
Malediction
Vermin ETC . . .

All the attributes above allow us to justify clearly who Satan is, the Evil one. In only two sentences we can also say that:

"Satan is the father of all viruses."
"Satan is the Prince of the hate."
"Satan is the god of Idiots."

℘ HOW DID GOD ACT?

Soon after, **God** saw that Lucifer was too artful. Then, **God** obliged to take strong sanctions against Lucifer such that: First, **God** put Lucifer out of heaven. Second, **God** condemned Lucifer to an eternal death penalty. Third, **God** has a day of judgement scheduled for Satan, and for all those who take part with Satan. Fourth, **God** acts to save us from the punishment.

Let's examine some good examples together, about the result of how the spread of Satan's virus begins to seriously emotionally impress the creations of **God**. For example, Satan made Adam and Eve refuse to obey to **God**. Satan made Cain kill his brother Abel with envy. For example, Satan caused Noah's people to sin and pushed **God** to destroy all these people, apart from Noah and his family. For example, Satan influenced the people of Sodom and Gomorrah to do wicked things under **God's** eyes; such as these, people committed adultery, homosexuality, ETC . . . Because of their actions, **God** destroyed Sodom and Gomorrah except for Lau and his family excluding his wife.

✎ TO STOP THE PROPAGATION OF SATAN'S VIRUS, WHAT DID GOD DO?

Because **God** loves us so much, he gave the life of his only son "**Jesus-Christ**" as a sacrifice to save us from this parasite named Satan. **Jesus-Christ** poured out his precious blood on the cross to save us, and **Jesus-Christ** came to give us more hope to go with him one day to live in his father's house in the heaven. However, Satan is looking to destroy our relationship with **Jesus-Christ**. **God** is waiting for the last day, on his schedule of judgement for Satan and all people who continue to follow the evil behavior of Satan. **God** will accomplish this by:

- And the devil that deceived them was cast into the lake of fire and brimstone, where the beast and the false prophet are, and shall be tormented day and night for ever and ever. Ref. **Revelation 20:10.**

- Then shall he say also unto them on the left hand, depart from me, ye cursed, into the eternal fire which is prepared for the devil and his angels. Ref. **Matthew 25:41.**

Again, examine some important examples about the same question of the difference between Heaven and Earth. On the first hand, heaven is where **God** is living with his son **Jesus-Christ**, the **Holy Spirit**, and the Angels. On the second hand, earth is where humans are living with Satan and his evil spirits. To become localized, **God** established his Holy Throne in heaven. The earth is the place of a violence and difficulty because it's under the power of humans and Satan.

Briefly, we just continue to see the difference between even the children of **God** and those of Satan. The children of **God** must be well dressed, distinguish from that of Satan's children. That means, the children of **God** must have all these qualities following as an agent of: justice, frank, love, and peace. At first, the children of **God** must be totally different; handsomely dressed, to talk, and to act. The children of **God** must be of exemplary for the correct conduct of the society, and for the Christian life. The children of **God** live with hope in **Jesus-Christ**, and they believe in only **God**, **Jesus-Christ**, and **Holy Spirit** hence they will live eternally with **God**. **God's children** are followers of **Jesus-Christ** who is our savior and **God's Son**.

Let's also examine how the children of Satan are so different from the children of **God**.

Satan's children are; malefactors, destroyers, full of hate, ambitious, hypocrites, liars, dishonest, enemies of Christians, friends of violence, tricksters, criminals, robbers, adulterous, blasphemers, slanderers, wicked, and everything bad.

We're already know, firstly, that Satan was created by God and lived with God in the heaven. Secondly, Satan was ambitious, he wanted to occupy his own powerful throne as God reigns in his throne. Satan refused to obey God, so, Satan used to make so many people to follow him.

Why Satan wanted people to follow him?

Satan knew that he doesn't have any more of opportunities to get back in heaven. He knew, the only and only thing that's left for him is "to burn in the eternal fire". So, Satan worked so hard every day and every night to have more people to go to burn with him in the eternal fire. It's also clear that, all these who walk under Satan's potentiality will lose the blessing of **God**, the eternal life that **Jesus-Christ** came to give to those who believe in him.

As a result, everybody can know **God's** plan now:

He put Satan out from his wonderful throne.

He had condemned Satan to burn in the eternal fire.

He will judge and condemn all who did not accept his son **Jesus-Christ** as their savior.

Right now, Satan gives himself the job of seducing as

much of people who live on the earth to go with him in the depths of hell eternally. Do you see how that Satan is a malefactor because he does not want to burn alone so he is looking to get more and more people to burn with him in the eternal fire. All these who allowed Satan to seduce them, will become Satan's children.

I want to ask you my friends:

Can you now make your choice and see the difference between Satan and **God**?

Who will go to live in **God**'s house eternally with **Jesus- Christ**?

Who will go to burn in the eternal hell with Satan?

Understand this very well my friend that you've to establish the difference between **God** and Satan now, before it's too late for you.

Listen to this now! This is the truth:

God is real,
God is Love,
God is Perfect,
Holy-Holy is only **God**,
God is our creator
and our true Father.
God is the eternal **God**!
God is the Beginning and the End
(Alpha and Omega).
If you come follow **Jesus-Christ**,
you'll have the grace of **God**,
so you'll have eternal life.

"These things have I written unto you that believe on the name of the **Son** of **God**; that you may know that you have eternal life, and that you may believe in the name of the **Son** of **God**." Ref. **1 John 5:13**.

On the other hand, please be careful and listen right now! This is the truth:

> Satan is a big liar,
> Satan is hateful,
> Satan is a false god,
> Satan is more inferior than a trash bag.
> Satan is a bad spirit.
> Satan is described in the **Bible**: "The great dragon was hurled down-that ancient serpent called the devil, or Satan, who leads the whole world astray. He was hurled to the earth, and his angels with him." Ref. **Rev. 12:9**.

Moreover, Satan is already condemned to burn in the eternal hell. This means that, you don't have to fear Satan or anyone who can kill only your body. Illustrated in this Biblical passage: "Do not be afraid of those who kill the body but cannot kill the soul. Rather, be afraid of the One who can destroy both soul and body in hell." Ref. **Matthew 10:28.**

That's serious, you must think about that. That means, if you follow Satan just because you fear of him, the result is: "You'll burn in the eternal Hell with him." Additionally, "And the devil that deceived them was cast into the lake of fire and brimstone, where the beast and the false prophet are, and shall be tormented day and night for ever and ever." **Revelation 20:10.**

☞ YOUR ONLY SOLUTION IS: "COME NOW!"

God loves you so much, don't look behind you. Come to **Jesus-Christ**." That means, if you follow **Jesus-Christ**, in addition, you'll have eternal life. **Jesus-Christ** said: "I am the way and the truth and the life. No one comes to the Father except through me." Ref. **John 14:6**.

Let's do a little analysis on the points that we are coming to develop:

Who is God?

Is there a difference between all that God has created?

Does God himself admit the difference in his creation?

It appears clear to see that **God** has really created nature with of all kinds of different of elements. Really all these different elements are the compounds of the nature, or life completely. They are translated for us with the magnificence of **God**'s glory.

That is reason of that we should say also that **God** show to us in all interpretation, in everywhere, and in all point, by approaching at his Common Denominator what is "Pure" that's toward the whole of these components of his Love: Handsomely, Universal. **God** had never created anything in life with any idea of superiority or of inferiority. That means, all that existed in **God**'s creation, are good and very important to explain how that He is: **"Wonderful, All Power, and Supreme Lord."** The Bible said: "For by him were all things created, that are in heaven, and that are in earth, visible and invisible, whether they be thrones, or dominions, or principalities, or powers: all things were created by him, and for him." Ref. **Colossians 1:16**.

Moreover, men must change their mentality, because men like to be ignorant of the greatest importance of this difference that exists between the elements in **God**'s creation. Indeed, it's possible to take one among the good examples such that of man and the animal to better demonstrate the existence and the role of the difference. **God** gave to man: Intelligence, the power over all the other creatures that are on the earth and the heavens. Then, the **Bible** explains to us what **God** said, "Let us make human beings in our image, to be like us. They will reign over the fish in the sea, the birds in the sky, the livestock, all the wild animals on the earth, and the small animals that scurry along the ground." Ref. **Genesis 1:26**.

Therefore, we can see that this is **God** himself who had established the difference of the superiority of man in regarding to the animal. At first, we can see that this is **God** who is our creator. This is God who is our "Supreme **Lord**".

Moreover, there is not a part in the Bible that tells us one group of man is superior to another group of man. The reason being all men came from **God**'s image, and however you look: the color, rich, poor, knowledge, ETC . . . In fact, all men have the same Father or the one **Supreme God**. And every man is created in **God**'s image, then we must all live as brothers and sisters.

It is our duty to love each other, and to glorify our **Supreme Father who is our God of Love**. We must glorify **God** for all this variety of things that He places in life with care for man to enjoy, fortify. We see for example, when each season is coming with of different of flowers, then that is doing to embellish the nature and **God**'s glory.

What appears a little problematic at the man's side it's that, instead of man surrendering all the glory to the **Lord**, especially; for each one of the different of things that **God** created, but so many people prefer to remain in ignorance with Satan. It's our ignorance of **God** that put us very far from the Divine power. In addition, we become falling in the suffering. Everybody wants to ask this question, if God's Love is incomparable but: **Where is the suffering coming from?**

One of the biggest links of suffering come from man on earth and is caused by the bad interpretation of the question, the "Difference between each of the elements that exist in **God**'s creation by the human."

Moreover, there is-it the difference the original of the suffering?

We may answer "No" to the question posed, because we already know that **God** is "**Holy**", that he's the creator of the universe. **God** is **Love**, **Holy**, **Powerful**, and **Generous**. What I want to say is that man and all those who try to understand the universe, are created by **God**. What's to say; all **God**'s works are unmingled. That they justify the magnanimity of **God**.

God knows how to decorate his board, He has placed different days and nights, as well as the nature of sweet or bitter fruits. Another example that we can observe, **God** is real, He has proven to us that He is the supreme **God** and only Master. The issue about the point we have, is to say that "**God** is the only **God**".

Then, we must talk about sins indeed; we directly observe "the impurity" that is completely against **God**'s plan. We believe that our **God** who should have never like to see us, or who should let us live in the suffering. That was the reason, **God** placed Adam and Eve in the garden where **God** used to put the paradise. Where, God provided everything for them including a wonderful life. "Now the **Lord God** had planted a garden in the east, in Eden; and there he put the man he had formed. 9) **The Lord God** made all kinds of trees grow out of ground- trees that were pleasing to the eye and good for food. In the middle of the garden were the tree of life and the tree of the knowledge of good and evil." Ref. **Genesis 2:8-9**.

Until now, there is no mention that the source of the

suffering was already active in **God's** administration for man or for Lucifer. But, before the situation changes for the worst for man, **God** exhorted the man. For example, the Bible states:"16. And the **Lord God** commanded the man "You are free to eat from any tree in the garden; 17. but you must not eat from the tree of the knowledge of good and evil, for when you eat from it you will certainly die." Ref. **Genesis 2:16,17.**

Let's calmly continue to search for the real answer that should help us to find the origin, or the cause of the suffering. Let's go right to the creation of Angels and Lucifer. **God** created all the Angels including Lucifer. All the Angels were so beautiful, but Lucifer was the most beautiful among them. Before the majesty of the Great Creator "**God**" all the Angels prostrate to adore, to glorify with so much joy. At the first, **God** gave to Lucifer so much power, knowledge, power to decide, and control the other Angels. So, Lucifer was called "Angel of Light". But, Lucifer was not happy to see that it was only for **God** that the Angels prostrate, glorify, adore, ETC . . . Lucifer wanted **God's** position, then he revolted against **God**. Read us this biblical passage:"12) How you are fallen, O Lucifer, son of the morning! How you are cut down to the ground, you who weakened the nations! 13) For you have said in your heart: I will ascend into heaven, I will exalt my throne above the stars of God; I will also sit on the mount of the congregation on the farthest sides of the north; 14) I will ascend above the heights of the clouds; I will be like the most High." Ref. **Isaiah 14:12-14.**

The first observation is, that after Lucifer revolted against **God** we can see now that Lucifer was the one who lays down the original pion of suffering. The actions of Lucifer exhibit: "Disobedience, Ambition or of Arrogance" against the Love, and the Greatness of **God**. Lucifer wanted to overthrow the **God's** power. Imagine, **God** is the one and only one creator of everything including the creation of Lucifer. That means, Lucifer could not create anything so, how is he going to live without **God's** creation? In addition, **God** put out Lucifer from the heaven. In fact, Lucifer caused his own fall. That is explained in this biblical passage:"13) You were in Eden, the garden of God; every precious stone adorned you: carnelian, chrysolite and emerald, topaz, onyx and jasper, lapis lazuli, turquoise and beryl. Your settings and mountings were made of gold; on the day, you were created they were prepared. 14) You were anointed as a guardian cherub, for so I ordained you. You were on the holy mount of God; you walked among the fiery stones. 15) You were blameless in your ways from the day you were created till wickedness was found in you. 16) Through your widespread trade you were filled with violence, and you sinned. So, I drove you in disgrace from the mount of God, and I expelled you, guardian cherub, from among the fiery stones. 17) Your heart became proud in the account of your beauty, and you corrupted your wisdom because of your splendor. So, I threw you to the earth; I made a spectacle of you before kings." Ref. **Ezekiel 28:13-17**.

We must continue to believe that "God's Love is Incomparable". In the same serenity, we're going to continue to search for the answer for the source of suffering. We already know that across the shadows at the field of the true word that is the **"Bible,"** where **God** teaches us about of his divine creation. Then, let's go expressly in the Garden of Eden where **God** has placed Adam and Eve. **God** created a great life for them, meaning, everything they needed was there for wonderful living conditions. There was all and all for living well in the Garden of Eden. Let's read this biblical passage together:"15) The LORD God took the man and put him in the Garden of Eden to work it and take care of it. 16) And the LORD God commanded the man, "You are free to eat from any tree in the garden; 17) but you must not eat the tree of the knowledge of good and evil, for when you eat from it, you will certainly die". Ref. **Genesis 2:15-17**.

Until now, we can see how that "God's Love is

Incomparable", He did not want that anything bad happen to Adam and Eve, God told them: Do not eat the tree of the knowledge of good and evil . . . The second observation that we can make, is the arrival of Satan on the Earth and the cunning serpent that lived in the garden of Eden, are then coming like there's a thunder about, and very stain of sins, and of maledictions. Thus, the Bible lets us know that, Adam and Eve were the first residents of the earth. They had a wonderful relationship with the Lord God. However, the Serpent became so jealous to see how **God** had taken care of Adam and Eve. Afterwards, Serpent used his guiles for fascinating Adam and Eve in making them eat the tree of knowledge that **God** forbid them to eat... The Bible states: "1) Now the serpent was most crafty than any of the animals the LORD God had made. He said to the woman, "Did God really say, 'You must not eat from any tree in the garden'?" 2) The woman said to the serpent, "We may eat fruit from the trees in the garden, 3) but God did say, 'You must not eat fruit from the tree that is in the middle of the garden, and you must not touch it, or you will die'." 4) "You will not certainly die," the serpent said to the woman. 5) "For God knows that when you eat from it your eyes will be opened, and you will be like God, knowing good and evil." 6) When the woman saw that the fruit of the tree was good for food and pleasing to the eye, and also desirable for gaining wisdom, she took some and ate. She also gave some to her husband, who was with her, and he ate it. 7) Then the eyes of both were opened, and they realized they were naked; so, they sewed fig leaves together and made covering for themselves. Ref. **Genesis 3:1-7**.

According to the Bible, all the holies exalt with vigor, in singing to the Holy God. It is written: "And they were calling to one another: "Holy, Holy, Holy is the Lord Almighty; the whole earth is full of his glory." Ref. **Isaiah 6:3**.

How shall Adam and Eve go to hold in God's face? Look at us that God is Love, Pure, and Holy. It is a fact that, in the

Splendor of his perfect love, of his perfect Holiness, manifest will totally render us happy. So, God has not one place for all that is unhealthy. This explain that Adam and Eve are already subject of the disobedience to God. Whereas, **God** is waiting for Adam and Eve this what is good but no more disobedience. The Bible said: "Do not conform to the pattern of this world but be transformed by the renewing of your mind. Then you will be able to test and approve what God's will is-his good, pleasing and perfect will." Ref. **Rom 12:2**.

This is the manner **God** has always used to the exhortation in his infinite kindness. Because he wanted to do all this for the prosperity of everyone. It is to say, **God** should not love and that he should never love any depraved things be it so arrived in his plan of work for everybody.

Moreover, that is one of the reasons that **God** can tell Adam and Eve not to eat the fruit of the tree. We see that Adam and Eve do not listen to **God** so, they fall to the punishments of their faults and oblige to **God** to take his measures limited with them. Let's see how that the Bible explains to us the last moment of meeting between the Eternal Lord, Adam and Eve in the garden of Eden: "8) Then the man and his wife heard the sound of the LORD God as he was walking in the garden in the cool of the day, and they hid from the LORD God among the trees of the garden. 9) But the LORD God called to the man, "Where are you?" 10) He answered, and I was afraid because I was naked; so, I hid." 11) And he said, "Who told you that you were naked" Have you eaten from the tree that I commanded you not to eat from?" 12) The man said, "The woman you put here with me-she gave me some fruit from the tree, and I ate it." 13) Then the LORD God said to the woman, "What is this you have done?" The woman said, "The serpent deceived me, and I ate." Ref. **Genesis 3:8-13**.

✆ THE CONSEQUENCES THAT MAY ARRIVE TO THE ONES THAT DO NOT LISTEN TO THE ETERNAL GOD'S VOICE.

At first, **God** wants to be the friend of the man that he has created. **God** presents himself as the protector of man. However, the man prefers to live in ignorance. What I want to say, that man arrive not to understand the importance, and the power of **God**. That is the same thing we see every time in our society. A good position job only may change man's mentality and make him to understand that he's the most important than another. We can understand for example, a president arrived to call other people from Africa, Haiti, and Venezuela bad word like that "shithole nations//Jan 11, 2018. It's sad, and it's so sad to hear that for a naïve president used to dismiss him as all brawn and no brain, really he did not know what God said: "Let us make mankind in our image, in our likeness, so that they may rule over the fish in the sea and the birds in the sky, over the livestock and all the wild animals, and over all the creatures that move along the ground." Ref. Genesis 1:26. That means, under God's Love everybody is equal.

How can we understand that, the woman Eve is seduced (fascinated) by the old-stupid and sly snake with solely a fruit that his creator, that is **God** had said not to eat for not to perish? God had stablished a sweet life, rich and eternal life for man. But, the moment that man became disobedient to God's order, everything changed. For example, the sweet life changed to suffering; deceased, detestable, delinquency, etc... What a terrible fall that man has taken. See us how that the Bible explains to us the fall of humanity, beginning with Adam and Eve: "14) so the LORD God said to the serpent, "Because you have done this, cursed are you above all livestock and all wild animals! You will crawl on your belly and you will eat dust all the days of your life. 15) And I will put enmity Between you and the woman, and between your seed and her seed; he shall bruise your head, and you shall bruise his heel." 16) To the Woman He said: "I will greatly multiply your sorrow and your conception; your desire shall be for your husband, and he shall rule over you." 17) Then to Adam He said, "Because you have heeded the voice of your wife, and have eaten from the tree of which I commanded you, saying, 'You shall not eat of it': "Cursed is the ground for your sake; In toil you shall eat of it all the days of your life. 18) Both thorns and thistles it shall bring forth for you, and you shall eat the herb of the field. 19) By the sweat of your brow you will eat your food until you return to the ground, since from it you were taken; for dust you are and to dust you will return." Ref. **Geneses 3:14-19**.

Whoever it may be Lucifer, serpent, Adam and Eve are falling in the disobedience and hunted from the heaven and from the garden of Eden, it is all result that the Eternal God stay and will stay the Supreme Eternal God. Because, "God's Love is Eternally good and strong". For example, He has continued to give to the man the possibility to live on the earth. But with a condition, that the man be it so, eating by the sweat of one's brow. Get us to read that biblical version: "22) Then the LORD God said, "Behold, the man has become like one of Us, to know good and evil. And now, lest he put out his hand and take also of the tree of life, and eat, and live forever" 23) therefore the LORD God sent him out of the garden of Eden to till the ground from which he was taken. Ref. **Genesis 3:22-23**.

After the disobedience of Adam and Eve everything became serious, that's to say; the motives that oblige to the LORD **God** to take his measures of limited backwards and forwards that's to say above all.

What's the most terrible case in life, when we listen to Satan and disobey the Eternal God. Sometimes, the man listens to Satan or to others to get riches or a better position or job. And sometimes, there are those who accept the offer of Satan, or offers from other persons in default of the fear of Satan or other people to not kill them. It is written in the Bible, this is God's word: "Do not be afraid of those who kill the body but cannot kill the soul. Rather, be afraid of the One who can destroy both soul and body in hell." Ref. **Matthew 10:28**.

God created us of two natures: The Flesh (human body) and the Spirit. Then, the difference between those two kinds of natures is, all those who act according to the human body, are more materialistic. On the other hand, all those who act according to the sprit, are more interested at the things that coming from heaven.

Refer to this Biblical version: "17 For the flesh desires what is contrary to the Spirit, and the Spirit what is contrary to the flesh. They are in conflict with each other, so that you are not to do whatever you want."
Ref. **Galatians 5:17**.

☞ ANALYZE TWO MORE EXAMPLES FOR BETTER TO MAKE CLEAR THE BIG DIFFERENCE BETWEEN THE FLESH AND THE SPIRIT.

Firstly, on the point of the flesh, there is a strength and weakness, above all in the moments of proofs, suffering, the conflicts, famines, difficulties, sickness, temptations, dead, persecution, etc... in a word, the flesh has not any resistance for fighting against the lusts (covetousness) or the strength by the sins. On the other hand, take the case of Adam and Eve. The serpent used the weakness of the flesh on Eve and then, Eve used the weakness of flesh on Adam. It is all result, they are seduced by the serpent that's where they fall under God's punishment. Today again, we see how that there are so many people who remain on the evil side. Those people act differently from Adam and Eve. However, they always act in the disobedience of God. To add some little details to better recognize Satan's believers, they are everywhere in the world, and whatever the color or race, rich or poor. We may know them across their acts such that:

Savage as the animal in the forest.

Deceitful, criminal, thief, drug-addict, evil or cruel magician, plotter.

Fraudulent in front of: Popular, State, Church, Family, Poor or

Rich, from any administration or foundation, organization

Public or social.

- Abortion: Women, doctors, nurses, charlatans or impostors.
- Adulterous, liar, Blasphemer, Prostitution, Homosexual.
- Materialists.
- Tempter of: Theft, crime, deceiver.
- Artful.
- Arrogant, jealous, ambitious.
- Unbecoming clothes, supernatural hair, false nails or dirty nails, silly person with crazy making up, wear a low dress.
- Avenger.
- Corrupting, association of malefactor.

Nevertheless, those forms of sins are qualified as the effects of the guiles from the evil for fascinating all that one walks and acts according to the flesh. The Bible tells us: "19) The acts of the flesh are obvious: sexual immorality, impurity and debauchery; 20) idolatry and witchcraft; hatred, discord, jealousy, fits of rage, selfish ambition, dissensions, factions 21) and envy; drunkenness, orgies, and the like. I warn you, as I did before, that those who live like this will not inherit the kingdom of God." Ref. **Galatians 5:19-21**.

Satan knew his destiny because he sinned against **God**, he is convicted to burn Eternally in the hell. In the same means, he did not want to burn alone. That's one of the reasons why he uses the points that are sensitive to the flesh such that: suffering, difficulty, misery, sickness, death, age, humiliation, conflict, famine, catastrophes, persecution, and all kinds of problems... just to captivate man to thus leading to disobedience of the Eternal God. Then, all those who are captivated by Satan's temptation as Adam and Eve because they are carnal, so they are going to burn with Satan in hell. Read this well-beloved biblical part: "Once I was alive apart from the law; but when the commandment came, sin sprang to life and I died." Ref. **Rom 7:9**.

℘ WOULD YOU RATHER FOLLOW SATAN AND DISOBEY GOD?

Before answering the question, it must first be determined: Who is Satan?

Satan is the enemy of God's works, such that; the nature, the man, even the Angels, so why not God also. In fact, Satan is showing up in everything and everywhere. For example, he's showing up in the society, the lover relationship, the family relationship, natural catastrophes, the events, the earthquake, the wars, the governments, the crimes, the diseases, accidents, etc... Satan pursues his objective that is to let us know that he is the strong power just, so he can change the direction of the people's belief in all the world that means not believe in God but in him. Listen that biblical version: "The great dragon was hurled down that ancient serpent called the devil, or Satan, who leads the whole world astray. He was hurled to the earth, and his angels with him." Ref. **Apocalypse 12:9**.

Satan did all that, while God himself already prepared: the day of judgement, the hell, and fix the special date to put an end to Satan. The disobedient angels, the devils, and all those who have chosen Satan for ignoring the Eternal God's existence, who is the creator of all the Universe.

I believe that no one would like to go to burn in hell with Satan the artful tormenting. The reason is that, when Satan is going to finish to make us to fall into temptation, that shall be again him that shall go to accuse us. Moreover, we'll be without of a defender from the day of judgment before **God**. Satan shall do us to know that he is one of ourselves to take the responsibility of our causes.

Secondly, on the point of the Spirit, Consider us before all the diverse temptations of Satan:

a) Job: The temptation of **Job**. In the two chapters of **Job 1-2** explain to us how Satan used his multiples tests for making to fall **Job**.

b) **David**: View that king **David** was haughty, Satan search to attract him: 1) Satan rose up against Israel and incited David to take a census of Israel 2) So David said to Joab and the commanders of the troops, "Go and count the Israelites from Beersheba to Dan. Then report back to me so I may know how many there are." Ref. **1 Chronicles 21**.

c) **Jesus-Christ**: Satan tempted **Jesus-Christ** as well. Then Jesus was brought by the Spirit in the desert, to be tempted by the evil. The **Bible** tells us everything, after forty days and forty nights, he was hungry. Let us examine together: "1) Filled with the holy Spirit, Jesus returned from Jordan and was led by the Spirit into the desert, 2) For forty days, to be tempted by the devil. He ate nothing during those days, and when they were over he was hungry. 3) And the devil said to him "If you are the **Son** of **God**, command this stone to become bread." Ref. **Luc 4:1-3**.

The serpent used the weakness of the flesh to try and seduce J**esus-Christ**. Besides, for **Jesus-Christ**, the flesh has no point of value.

The Spirit, that is in **Jesus-Christ**, is most firm than the flesh.

Jesus-Christ already knew the faking of Satan that is the base on the weakness of the flesh to tempt man.

According to the Holy scriptures, the Bible:

3) regarding his Son Who as to his earthy life was a descendant of David,

4) and who through the Spirit of holiness appointed the Son of God in power by his resurrection from the dead: Jesus Christ our Lord,

5) Through him we received grace and apostleship to call all the Gentiles to the obedience that comes from faith for his name's sake.

6) And you also are among those Gentiles who are called to belong to **Jesus Christ**.

7) To all in Rome who are loved by God and called to be his holy people: Grace and peace to you from our Father and from the LORD Jesus Christ." Ref. **Romans 1:3-7**.

Jesus-Christ proves oneself again, He is stronger than Satan.

Listen carefully to how **Jesus-Christ** answered to him:

4) **Jesus-Christ** answered, "It is written: 'Man shall not live on bread alone, but on every word, that comes from the mouth of God." Ref. **Matthew 4:4**.

Jesus-Christ answered him, "It is also written: Do not put the **Lord** your **God** to the test." Ref. **Matthew 4:7**.

It's also clear to see that God himself established the difference between the flesh and the spirit. For instance, the disobedience of Adam and Eve who had been let to charm by Satan who had the power of sin and death, is one of the big examples we can take for the flesh. Then, God became very unhappy, he excluded all of them from the Garden Eden. By contrast, Jesus-Christ came to clean our sins, he abolished death: but it has now been revealed through the appearing of our Savior, Christ Jesus, who has destroyed death and has brought life and immortality to light trough the gospel. Ref. **2 Timothy 1:10**. Jesus-Christ left for us the power of the Spirit of God. Right now, we are free by the blood of Jesus-Christ. The Spirit of God can help us to chase away Satan. In result, we can exclude Satan just to make our God happy as Jesus-Christ used to make happy his Father God when He excluded Satan over "And a voice from heaven, saying, this is my beloved Son, in whom I am well pleased." Ref. **Matthew 3:17;** Ref. **Matthew 17:5.**

It's really, all those that walk according the flesh shall be judged, condemned, and shall be burned in the hell eternally with Satan.

Passing from mouth to mouth; we must announce the good news of Jesus-Christ! So that we may help people to steer clear of the punishments pointed out above. At first, we must change the condition of our life. That means, we need to keep our heart ready. Because we live until today so far of God's order. This is the reason, we are sick physically and spiritually. The sins make us down, poor, smell bad, and very ugly before God. On the other hand, we must fight, using all our efforts for fighting against this weakness of the flesh that is in us.

✑ HOW ARE WE GOING TO FIGHT?

At first, we must know that we are weak, that means our choices do not always correspond to **God**'s voice. "19) For the good that I would I do not: but the evil which I would not, that I do. 20) Now if I do that I would not, it is no more I that do it, but sin that dwelleth in me." Ref. **Romans 7:19-20**.

So, we can see that our Eternal God doesn't take any pleasure in sin. It is not good that we live in sin. Everyone who chooses to live in the sin is Satan's child.

However, everyone who does fight against sin, is on their way to meet **Jesus-Christ** who is our Savior and who is going to bring us to God's house. Yes, what is necessary for us to know:

1) We are the descendants of Adam and Eve, so we are all sinners before God.

2) After that, you ought to come soon to receive pardon from God. This is what the Bible says: "**For all have sinned and come short of the glory of God.**" Ref. **Romans 3:23**.

We must take this choice seriously, for it is the only way that can obtain eternal life. Because, God himself had gave us the blood of his Only Son "Jesus-Christ" to wash away all our sins and that if we believe in him, we'll have everlasting life. In fact, if we come to Jesus-Christ, we will have the power for fighting against the temptations of Satan.

Despite all, God has had pity on us, he sent his only son Jesus-Christ for paying the debts of our sins with his blood. Now, enough that we believe only in him for that we don't fall under the anger of God. To continue fighting against the temptations of Satan, we must:

1) Do everything in our effort according the desires of the Spirit of God. It's only with the Spirit of God that we can follow Jesus-Christ, to fight the desires of the flesh, which is the craft of Satan.

2) Personally, accept Jesus-Christ as your Savior. According to the Bible: "For by grace are you saved through faith; and that not of yourselves: it is the gift of God. 9) Not of works, lest any man should boast. Ref. **Ephesians 2:8-9**; moreover, "It does not, therefore, depend on human desire or effort, but on God's mercy." Ref. **Romans 9:16**.

Be obedient to the word of God: We need the nourishment: **"All kinds of Food"** each day for our **flesh**. It is all one, we need of the nourishment: **"Word of God"** each day for our **Spirit**. Especially because the **"Word of God"** will grow our faith, and the good relationship with God. The **"Word of God"** is absolutely the tap-root of the faith. In order that we can have success with our faith in God, we must ruminate the **"Word of God"** at once and daily in the perseverance or in the proof of life just to prove to all the world:

- How wonderful God is. For the perseverance of the faith in the **"Word of God"** allows us to better understand the love that God has for us.

- The "**Word of God**" shall illuminate our belief with performance of good ideas to follow Jesus-Christ and rejected the bad ideas of temptations of Satan so far from us.
- The Bible gives us of good examples of how the "**Word of God**" has established a narrow communication between man and God, very comparable to God's relationship with Abraham, Jacob, Job, Moses, David etc...
- The "**Word of God**" is a perfect arm. It's has not his equal. It strengthened our perseverance in God. The result of his application is "the direct communication with God through the medium of our **Savior Jesus-Christ**.

When we use this perfect arm, the "**Word of God**", we will always be victorious. Let us take two examples from the Bible for clarification:

a) a) The victory of Little David over Goliath:"....". Ref. **1 Samuel 17:51**.

b) b) The victory of Moses over the strong army of Pharaoh: Ref. **Exodus 14.**

- We could considerer the relationship with God as a reservation primordial and to have as much of benefits or of eternal happiness. The Bible says: "To them who by patient continuance in well doing seek for glory and honor and immortality, eternal life." Ref. **Romans 2:7; Galatians 6:8-9**.

Until now, we can perceive how Satan is the biggest tempter according to the "**Word of God**". The Bible illustrates so many examples to us: Satan tempted Adam and Eve. Satan tried to tempt Job, David, even Jesus-Christ, to point out the best examples. They are great lessons that guide us on how we may resist against the temptations of Satan and how that we may totally mistrust Satan. For example, Jesus-Christ has been strong enough to put Satan far away from him. He proved his Love for us: From his birth, to his death on the cross, until to his final and major victory of his resurrection at the tomb. Then, washing us with his pure blood, he's making us free by breaking the chain of ours sins. In result, Jesus-Christ is showing to us what way to defeat Satan. And Jesus-Christ is coming to give us the power to also put Satan far away from us.

Satan does not have character, it has not dignity. Satan is the spirit of malicious, devouring, and cruelty. He shows that the division, the feud, the sadness. He is the spirit of destructor. He hasn't any truth in him. This is the reason that Jesus-Christ treated Satan like this: "You belong to your father, the devil, and you to carry out your father's desires. He was a murderer from the beginning, not holding to the truth, for there is no truth in him. When he lies, he speaks his native language, for he is a liar and the father of lies". Ref. **John 8:44**.

In the end, it is exactly from Satan himself that the origin of the suffering arises. Because it is from him that came the virus sin that corrupts humanity from generation to generation.

We are going now to bring some concrete ideas just to come to an end over each point that we come to develop above:

WHO IS GOD?

> God is the Alpha and the Omega
> The beginning and the end.
> He is the creator of the universe.

He is the creator of all the things that are in the universe.

He is the creator of all the things that we can see.

He is the creator of all the things that we can't see.

He is God of all the knowledges.

He is the one God who wants to share all goods and wealth.

He gives us the good senses: See - Smell - To understand - To touch

-To think - To breathe - To eat - To work - To rest - and to enjoy to all wonders.

*It doesn't exist, or it shall never exist another God as you my God!

WE MUST LOVE GOD.

God is the Holy and Right Father. He likes all his children. He takes of good care of his children and He protects his children. That is why He creates all and all for that everyone can be happy. Specially, God turns his hand to everything just to bring his Support on time and anytime for everybody whatever the situation and for whatever our needs.

It doesn't exist, or it shall never exist another God as you my God!

WE MUST LOVE GOD

God is watching us anywhere we are. Moreover, God puts his watchful Angels about his children. No one can hide under

God's eyes. The reason is, He penetrates from top to bottom at the heart, thought. He sees everywhere.

It doesn't exist, or it shall never exist another God as you my God!

WE MUST LOVE GOD

God is wonderful.
God is right and good.
God is Abraham's God,
God is Jacob's God,
God is of Moses's God,
God is Israel's God,
and, God is
God of every people on the earth,
all as God is
God of all the Angels in the heaven.

It doesn't exist, **or it shall never exist another God as you my God!**

WE MUST LOVE GOD

God is Love.
God is Sensible and Tender.
God has of Compassion for all his children.
God has of Goodness, of Wisdom, and of Mercy.
God has a quick ear for listening the prayer of or the yell of his
children. And, He answers the request of everybody.

ALL THE GLORY IS TO GOD

God reigns with eternal Extent.
God governs without difference.
God governs with the forgiveness.
God governs with the patience.
God governs with the freedom for everyone.
God doesn't make of distinction of nobody.
Whatever the color of man.
Whatever the level of knowledge.
Whatever poor or rich.
God treated us with respectful.
God has that one and same heart for all these
children.

ALL THE GLORY IS TO GOD

It doesn't exist and that it shall exist never another true democrat and a true governor as you my Lord!

Does Exist of the difference between all those that God created?

We would be a few absurd to not answer this question. Because, all appear clear under ours eyes at about of how that all go in the creation of God. Without any back thought, we would able to see that all the things that compose the whole of component parties of God's creation are beautiful, wonderful, and inexplicable. But in all these things, it exists well a big difference between them. We are going to take only one example for better make a complete comparison enough balance with most ample of lights between: Man and Lion.

℘ IN COMPARISON WITH MAN AND LION:

The man and the Lion, are two dominant elements among the most dominants elements of beings in the nature.

At first, God created the man to his image. He gave the intelligence to the man for that he can dominate over all the beings.

That explains that the man can act with reason. When a man is well behaved in the society, often we hear to say the people about him: That he's a man sociable, that he's a man who knows to reflect, that he's a moral man, that he's a Christian that's to say he's a man of God, etc... on the other hand, when a man is to misbehave in the society, then we hear to say the people about him: That he's a man no-sociable and all that is the contrary means he's a Satan's man, etc...

On the other hand, we see the Lion. God created the lion. That's one of the beast the stronger, the most dangerous, and the most wicked among the beasts that live in the nature, specially, in the forests.

The lion is beside himself with knowledge to think, or to reason. That's to say that the lion acts always instinctively. The lion kills and eats the flesh of all the other beasts, and same his similar. In fact, the aliments of the lion are: the flesh or dead body of the other beasts, all without exception including the man. Brief, seeing that the lion acts instinctively, in that case, it is well the subject for accomplishing at any bad thing or at any well thing without any thinking of judgment or punishment against him. In one word, the lion's act shall have longer to pursue or shall have no longer to pursue.

We're going to stand out the man's action in weight and in measure for better stablishing his difference in proportion of the lion's action. Let see one of the definition of the word Act that is well defined by Merriam-Webster. (https://www.merriam-webster.com/dictionary/act)

a) the doing of a thing: DEED. **an act of courage**

b) **law: something done voluntarily**

In the same way, that God created the man and gave him of the intelligence for dominate over all. But, that did not prevent man from bad action (to the exception of some) that should be not different to the acts of lion. The man did not use this big privilege 'brilliance' that God gave to him. That so be it well or bad, we can believe in this, there exist a similitude between those two opponents at the point of view "Cruel". This is not without reason that it does exist so thousands of courts of justice in the world completely, this is for saying clearly that the man is also cruel all as the lion.

But, whereas the man can use his consciousness to reason, then after to have exercised bad against the desire of his creator God, in fact it shall be judged and even to punish. At first sight, the man knew well already his situation that's to say if he is guilty or not by his perception that puts him in first place that's in himself, in second place, his consciousness puts him in the face of the society. And in the last place, the man's consciousness shall put him always in the face of his disobedience against God. Attention!!! " We must not forget that, it's Satan that gave birth to the stupid. This is not without reason that God has created the man with the intelligence, this is just to allow to the man to reject Satan without difficulty with all his traps, his bad ideas, and his disobedient action against God.

How can we understand that the man arrives to adore idols (statues), man kills his alike, he practices the bad in everything he's doing and in everything that he's saying, he practices the magic, the sorcery, he blasphemes the name of God. It looks like he doesn't have no fear about anything because he has the power and the money. For example, he has power even over the justice. Learn to us that well my dear friend/s... that it is most easy to be free at the court of justice from here below than to be free at God's court of justice. Because for the greater part of big stupid (Satan's servant) they use their diabolical power on their intelligence to give up for money the justice of others at the wicked that have of money or according to the good relationship or same stupid between them. That is why, whatever rich they may be, they take steps of drastic measures that have been writing in the documents at the court from here below to limit or punish the bad acts of the stupid despite that they are: criminals, exploiters, blasphemers, etc. However, they make free the stupid people most easy than the little unfortunate. At first, the judges from here below can also be disturbed to the attestation often roguishness of makers to the acts. The reason is the judges could not see inside of the public prosecutor's heart. Then, we could believe that the judges here below are limited for taking the true or justifiably decision.

It is very important to note that the judgement of man shall arrest not totally to the courts of the earth. Because, in the judgements courts of the earth by man, often the strong of the justice, the truth does not really reign. Where any who is from accused, could be free despite he/she is guilty. On the other hand, any who is from accused, could be condemned too despite he/she could be the guiltless. So many different reasons can explain that situation: For example, the humans are the judges, the corruption, money, the discrimination.

1) <u>The humans are the judges</u>: They can't see anything in the man's heart to discover the side there is untruth or the reality.

2) <u>The corruption</u>: So, certain judges decide to make the wrong person to be the winner in a contest for money. That means, they sale the justice of the guiltless to the guilty just because they have their specific reason. For

examples, these certain judges use for interest, they have love, or they protect sometime the relationship they have with the guilty person.

3) Money: So, certain judges are rendering the justice at where they see the most money.

4) So, certain judges are so plunged in the corruption, they do the discrimination, they protect their race of color in putting the biggest records of their guilty people in the oversight. They protect the fraudulent people. So, the unfortunate people are at 90% guilty to the courts from the entire world. This is one of reasons, we see often that many of people oblige to find justice for themselves. All these translate at sight the man's action, to let oneself be influenced by Satan's deceits.

✎ IN FACT, WHAT ARE YOU DOING WITH THE INTELLIGENCE THAT GOD HAD GAVE TO YOU?

The big relations, the richness, all the knowledge, and power of there below, the Satan's ruses, the fraudulent friends, etc... all of them shall not have any matter for that you use at the day of the judgment of God. As soon as God gave you of the intelligence, this is for that you can do that what is well, for that you can choose your real God and to reject Satan with all his liar at far from you. **The justice of God will be for everybody**. Then, rich or poor, judge, barrister/pleader, the accused/prisoner/defendant, illiterate, learned/well-informed, lawyer, authority, **everybody in general we will present in front of God's court of justice to judge from.** Person should not be able either to lead a scheduled lifestyle or to deceive God, because our heart is in the God's power hand daily. At first, the job of the heart is to remember everything that we're doing in our life: Well or Bad.

Don't mention it to liar. The lie shall make grow up more lies. If you don't cease to lie you will throw totally in the same line with the dirty beast that call 'Satan'. Then, God's eyes see whatever your activities everywhere, anywhere, and anytime. So, what are you going to do to defend yourself in front of the God's court of justice to be judged from?

It is written in the **Holy Bible**: "For we must all appear before the judgment seat of Christ, so that each of us may receive what is due us for the things done while in the body, whether good or bad." Ref. **2 Corinthians 5:10**.

NB: "But if you will not do so, behold, you have sinned against the Lord: and be sure your sin will find you out". Ref. **Numbers 32:23**

℘ HOW CAN WE GO AWAY OF THE SIN?

Being a sinner, you must:

1) Conform your heart according to God's desire: "Above all else, guard your heart, for everything you do flows from it." Ref. **Proverbs 4:23**.

2) Confess your sins in front of God for that your heart be it so clean:

   "Whoever conceals their sins does not prosper,
   but the one who confesses and renounces
   them finds mercy." Ref. **Proverbs 28:13**.

3) And like did David: "Then I acknowledged my sin to you and did not cover up my iniquity. I said, "I will confess my transgressions to the LORD." And you forgave the guilt of my sin. Ref. **Psalm 32:5**.

4) Believe in only **Jesus-Christ** as your Savior. Because, this is **Jesus-Christ** who had accepted to pour his "Precious Blood" on the cross just to clean up us. So that we can be free of the sin. And this is in Jesus-Christ's hands! that our solid relation comes to stablish with his "Father of Celestial God". Keep this in our memory: "In whom we have boldness and access with confidence by the faith of him." Ref. **Ephesians 3:12**.

5) Remove you of all the bad companionships (rich or poor) who are: treacherous, ruses, liars, spy, wicked, ambitious, thief, avaricious, kidnap, plotter, low intriguer, bad-tempered, impudicity, pornography, hate, egoism, anger, racism, Anti-Semitism, abject, covetousness and of all kinds in order that you do not fall in the sins with them. Listen what the Bible said: 11) Likewise reckon you also yourselves to be dead indeed unto sin, but alive unto God through Jesus-Christ our Lord. 12) "Let not sin therefore reign in your mortal body, that you should obey it in the lusts there of." Ref. **Romains. 6:11-12**.

6) Let your life in the powerful hand of "**Jesus-Christ**" in order that you may be an instrument of God. "Neither yield your members as instruments of unrighteousness unto sin: but yield yourselves unto God, as those that are alive from the dead, and your members as instruments of unrighteousness unto God." Ref. **Romains. 6:13**.

7) Do not torment yourself for the richness of the earth. Look first all the Kingdom of heaven. "But seek first his kingdom and his righteousness, and all these things will be given to you as well." Ref. **Matthew 6:33**.

8) Do not torment yourself with those who abuse you unjustly. "19) For this is thankworthy, if a man for conscience toward God endure grief, suffering wrongfully. 20) For what glory is it, if, when ye be buffered for your faults, ye shall take it patiently? but if, ye take it patiently, this is acceptable with God." Ref. **1 Peter 2:19-20**.

9) Finally, it must stay in the prior and walk in the sanctity for that the Holy Spirit of God be it so lived in you eternally.

Pay attention in all that you do in your life. As soon as you begin to do a sin, leave it in immediately. The reason is that, the sin introduces to sins.

If you do not return yourself at the traps of the first sin, then you should be familiarized with a chain of sins that should direct you to the throne of Satan.

Details:

You have finished to do the sin #1;
You liar for covering the sin #1 = sin #2;
You accuse of other to cover sin #2 = sin #3;
You're going to do all kinds of demagogies, the violence, crime just to
destroy your bad records sin #3 = You will become a master of sin = slave of Satan's throne.

℘ WHAT'S THAT GOD IS WAITING OF US?

Drag us on some main points to make clear better firstly, why that" The Love of God is Incomparable". We are going across depth and in the Immensity of the God's source of Love.

1) In God's creation, there are a variety of things. Let us take some examples: The sea, the river, the tree, the stars, the sun, the moon, the animals etc... God put all of them just for contemplate himself at first, after for displaying his Magnificence, whence all his works are perfectly Goods and Wonderful. God has disposed all to render happy all the elements that are in his creation. Moreover, God has put in his works all a variety of colors for better translate or explain the diversity that is in his big Love.

2) In God's creation, there is man with all a variety of languages, races and of different colors. Surrounded of all plenitude of ideas from whom can plough everywhere and elsewhere until the extremity of planetary. That means, God's Love allows the man to think freely and without limits.

3) In God's creation, there are the animals. Each of them has his own language, only manner to walk, to eat, to sleep, etc... But all the animals are created by God for contemplate himself, afterwards for that man may rejoice.

4) This is the Love of God which is Greatest which allow to God's nature to stay always with a wet paint, appears on our eyes of magnificent boards and faultless across all the horizons. From there, the Love of God allows us to discover how that our Supreme Creator is so remarkable in his manner. In fact, his Genius is unique though he is universal and incomparable.

5) The power of God's Love dominated on all the nations of the earth with so much of Wisdom and of Sharing. There is no speck of racism, no point of antisemitism, and point of the spirit of egoism. His most big order is: "This is my commandment, You Love each other, as I have Loved you." Ref. **John 15:12**.

6) The Love of God has not measure and has no price. The Love of God is stronghold, as prove; that He has gave in sacrifice the life of his unique Son Jesus-Christ just for putting up of the sin. What about Jesus-Christ's Blood allows us to have the mercy of God which is "The eternal life". What's again important to note: "The Love of God gave to all the world without any differentiation of races, of colors, rich or poor the same mercy and the same power of Gospel".

Amen-Amen-Amen ...God's Love is infinite. God's Love is Incomparable.

"God's Love is Incomparable", explains us very well, how and why that God use his power with love just to make the perfect, the beauty in everything that He finished to create. God doesn't put the different between everything to mean that each one has most value than another. However, it is a big opportunity that God gives to us that means, He just wants everybody to know how He is wonderful, how He has all power to do everything.

In fact, the society in each culture used that big opportunity that God give to us very bad. Like we may see the rich people or the knowledge people are living in different and best area than the poor people. For example, we may see how certain people use to say that they are most superior than other people just for a reason of different language, or different color, or even different culture of where people are coming from in a different country. On the other hand, people put out totally the value of equality of each one in the society. I believe that is one of the good reasons that the writer Cristie M. Locsin on the Role Her Filipino Heritage Played in Writing The value of Equality just to describe how people in 1969, put out her awesome book: the powerful hacienderos in the province of Azusa had been known to create politicians. The hacienderos who desired to keep their land and abolish the rebels groomed Mayor Karlos Vasquez to e ... (Publication January 30, 2017 by Publisher: Authorhouse)

It is very clear to see that once there is the question of inequality in any society the result is always like that: violence, injustice, fighting, misery for majority of people, exploitation of the weak people, bad administration, selfish people, revolution, crime, because people don't accept the different between of them. That explains also the augmentation of hatred and no sensibility, no charity at all. Listen what God said to us: "Love your neighbor as yourself. There is no commandment greater than these." Ref. Mark 12:31 The second.

NB: Satan himself does the diversion to change the direction of man's intelligence to stay in the ignorance until the deformation of the Width of God's Love.

Now, we must reject so far of our society all the idiotic (absurd) ideas of differentiation between us. Because, "In the Field of God's Love we are all "One" by the blood of our savior Jesus-Christ who unify us to become "His brother, Children of a same father who is God".

So, what that God is waiting from us now is: the humility between us, come to accept in our life his Dear Son "Jesus-Christ" as being our savior so that be we so pure to become to him like his well-loved children. What that we must reassemble as of brothers and sisters in the name of Jesus-Christ for praying him and to render him glory all the time and only that to him only. He is waiting from us: "a change of Love in our heart for each other".

That be we so sensible, charitable, live us together. At last, testify to the truth of God's Love everywhere, how that the Love of God is Great, how that the Love of God is Incomparable.

This is the reason that we keep saying everywhere and anytime that: "All the glory is for Eternal God. Halleluiah!!!! Amen.

My Soul is proud to exalt your Love oh my God like that: Your Love is so Great!

> Oh God, you are so Great!
> All those that you have did
> are totally perfects.
> In the source of your Love that we can really
> find all.
> Your Love gives me the joy
> and it did to shine on me
> all the Splendor
> of your Grace.
> Oh yes Lord ...
> of all my heart,
> I ask you
> to change this world
> bring us out
> the strong of your Love.
> Thousands of thanks
> For life ...
> of your only Son Jesus-Christ
> that you gave in sacrifice
> for that he can purify us
> and for that he can save us
> Thank you!!!
> Thousands of thanks
> Your powerful Love

that you have for us
You gave us the hope
You guided us steps by steps
You gave to us a big victory
on Satan that has any power.
God's Love rested on those who believe in him:
A powerful light
A source of life
a strengthening of nourishment
a serum anti-sin
Stronger than the hate
Hunter of the pain
Protection in everything
a bosom friend
an arm infallible
an invisible protection
an arm without equal
Yes...
"The Love of God is Incomparable."

11) Yours, Lord, is the greatness, and the power, and the glory and the majesty and the splendor, for everything in heaven and earth, is yours. Yours, Lord, is the kingdom, you are exalted as head over all. 12) Wealth and honor come from you; you are the ruler of all things. In your hands are strength and power to exalt and give strength to all". Ref. **1 Chronicles 29: 11-12**.

I want to invite all of you to take part immediately at this big meeting to God's house where that you and I are going to live for eternally and hopefully to the spread of this "Incomparable Love of God". Jesus-Christ is on his way to come back. Jesus-Christ will go with us to his Father God's house. Come fast my brothers and my sisters to do the reservation of your ticket. Yes, you must decide right now before it's too late. Because there will be a big adversity that God reserve for all those who have been rejected his Son Jesus-Christ. The big adversity is: the eternal burn/hell for Satan and for all those who rejected Jesus-Christ. If you do not accept Jesus-Christ in your life, then you'll not have the invitation to go to God's house.

Please remember that:

1) Love of God is free.

2) Jesus-Christ already gave his blood on the cross just to make us free under Satan.

3) Jesus-Christ payed the price of our ticket to go to God's house. Then, what are you waiting to do now?

The safety and the security of your life are the greatest concern at "The Incomparable Love of God". On the other hand, the adversity and suffer of your life are the greatest concern at Satan. So, decide by yourself the good way to take. That means, you have before you two ways that are: 1) Accept Jesus-Christ. Result, you'll go to the eternal life with Jesus-Christ and the Angels to God's house. 2) Accept Satan. Result, you'll go to burn with Satan in the eternal hell.

I dedicate my book to everyone especially to:

- ❖ Eng. Rose Laure JeanPhilippe
- ❖ Whens JeanPhilippe
- ❖ Wisslaure JeanPhilippe
- ❖ Mr. Pierre JeanPhilippe
- ❖ Mme. Analia JeanPhilippe
- ❖ Rev. P. JeanClaude JeanPhilippe
- ❖ Rev. P. Fritz JeanPhilippe
- ❖ Fritzlee JeanPhilippe
- ❖ Veronique Johnson
- ❖ Mondy JeanPhilippe

- ❖ Rood Falex Joseph
- ❖ Marnelle Laguerre
- ❖ Johnson Laguerre
- ❖ Djimy Biene
- ❖ Louimene Bonnet
- ❖ Caelle Edmond
- ❖ Yves Pierre Louis
- ❖ Nedjie Alfrena
- ❖ Hogarth Sankara Henry
- ❖ Jems Ferdinand
- ❖ Claude Enefort
- ❖ Hugues Mercier
- ❖ Fresnel Cobite
- ❖ Rosena Llieno
- ❖ RoseLourde Rene
- ❖ Nicolson Nasri Petit
- ❖ Kenson JeanLouis
- ❖ Jean Michel
- ❖ JeanLouis Jack Odson
- ❖ Gladys Belneau
- ❖ James Alfrena
- ❖ Nicole Geffrard Nervaud
- ❖ Debra McIntyre
- ❖ Beana Amilcar
- ❖ Darling Beethoveline Pierre
- ❖ Fabrice Hollant
- ❖ Francoise Biene
- ❖ Kimberley Lemons
- ❖ Jean Denis Leger and family
- ❖ Guirlene Jonas and family
- ❖ Cassandra Petit
- ❖ Jean Claude Germain
- ❖ Guy Anselme
- ❖ Lucina Jean Mildor
- ❖ Rodachsly Joseph

- ❖ Magalie Beaucejour
- ❖ Jospite Thoby
- ❖ Jean Cadet Roemo and family
- ❖ Laura Feliciano
- ❖ Shreen Azmy
- ❖ Nicolas Assoumou
- ❖ Patricia Gonzales
- ❖ Mirlande Michel
- ❖ Derrick Hutchinson
- ❖ Jean Emile Thevenin
- ❖ Pierre Louis Frederic (Fredo Kanpech)

jpw

ABOUT THE AUTHOR

1) The reason why I am qualified to write the book is because of the imagination that I have and the experiences I went through. I always feel the presence of God around me, he is my true creator.

2) Writing books is a fun hobby for me to express my imagination about life.

3) I live in United States of America, in Nashville, TN, and I enjoy the nature around me. I also enjoy planting.

Printed in the United States
By Bookmasters